10% of All Author Proceeds Will Be Donated
To Educational Non-Profits

Thru in 2

The Guide to Finishing College on Time (Or Even Early) and Saving Thousands in the Process

Mike Wilson

January 1, 2008

Visit
www.ThruIn2.com
For more resources, information and purchasing options

ISBN: 978-0-6151-9024-2

CONTENTS

INTRODUCTION

About Thru in 2

Get on the phone and call your family members, your spouse, your friends, or even the college of your dreams and ask them this question: "How many years will it take for me to earn a bachelor's degree?" You will, almost certainly receive the following answer: *"Four years."* It is a very standard assumption that a bachelor's degree from a reputable college should take *"four years."* Hence, the desire to earn a bachelor's degree at a "four year college" versus earning an associate's degree from a "two year college."

Prepare yourself. I have sad and shocking news. According to the National Center for Education

Statistics, 1 out of every 3 (33.3%) college students will actually finish in four years. Allow me to repeat it. Less than 33.3% of the students entering college in any given year will actually finish their degree in four years. The majority of students will take five to six years to complete their degree.

These shocking statistics are not because students are less prepared or even less capable than they once were. High school graduates in the 21st century are actually much more capable and mentally prepared than graduates twenty, ten, or even five years ago. The real cause of this nationwide educational constipation lies in the institutions themselves. The post-secondary educational system is structured in a manner that makes it extremely difficult for ANY student to graduate in four years.

With untrustworthy college "advisors," paper work that needs an enigma machine to decipher, and the total hours to complete a degree that just does not add up to "four years," ladies and gentleman, the odds really are against you.

I am living, breathing, contemporary proof that it is possible to obtain a college degree in four years, three years, or even two years all while enjoying the college experience and living life to the fullest. I, Mike Wilson, Shawnee Mission South high school graduate of 2003, with a national average IQ, an ACT score of 19, a GMAT score of 540 and no advanced placement credits to my name, finished my undergraduate degree from the University of Kansas (KU) in just TWO years. I then went on to earn my Masters in Business Administration (MBA) from the University of Missouri – Kansas City in just ONE year (2006).

To put this into perspective, when all of my friends were juniors at their respective colleges, I was graduating with my Masters in Business Administration from a top 10 entrepreneurship school. The great part is, I saved $150,849 by doing so. In tangible terms, that's comparable to purchasing almost three BMW convertibles. Given the time that it takes an average college student to obtain earn an equivalent degree, that is a savings of $4,190.25 a school week or

$838.05 a school day. The most interesting part of all is that I not only saved money, but I had a blast while doing it.

All it takes is a little motivation, a little hard work and knowing the ins and outs of the post-secondary educational system. No enigma machine required. Fortunately, you picked up this book, which is the first step to taking control of your college education and not only saving yourself a few hundred migraines and sleepless nights, but a few thousand dollars as well.

With the help of a motivating mother and a little ambition, I have successfully navigated the turbulent waters of college and saved an astronomical amount of money in the process. In turn, I am providing YOU with the ins, outs, secrets, tips, and resources necessary for you to finish your degree on time, or even early.

Read this book and apply its contents. It could be the best investment you ever make.

It All Started With a 1987 Corvette

My Motivation – A 1987 Corvette

For me, it all started with a fixer-upper 1987 Corvette. Sounds like an extravagant birthday present for a 16 year old in Johnson County, Kansas, but this Corvette changed my life forever. This Corvette was the front door that led me to the gates of success that I stand by today. Listen closely, as the story just gets more interesting from here on out.

My father has a good friend that owns a salvage yard in Little Rock, Arkansas, and coincidently was trying to sell a used, high mileage, black 1987 Corvette right around my sixteenth birthday. My father and I flew down to Arkansas to take a look at it and see if there were any major problems. That very same day, I drove home from Little Rock, Arkansas, to Overland Park, Kansas in a sweet, used 1987 Corvette.

This Corvette had its fair share of issues, and ironically, for that very reason, my father suggested it as my 16th birthday present. My parents bought me a fixer-upper car in order to provide me with a constructive outlet for my time. Believe it or not, in suburban USA, too many kids, have too much money and too often go down the wrong path. I was at a ripe and impressionable age that could have easily parlayed into a very different life from than the one I have today. Hanging out with the wrong friends, or going to the wrong party, or being in the wrong situation and I could have spawned into a very different person. My parents pledged to keep me away from that lifestyle.

Sure enough, their plan worked. I thought I was the coolest kid on the block with a $7,500 Black 1987 Corvette. The vehicle looked like the Batmobile and people thought I was Batman. I quickly found that so many people were asking me about my car (what kind of engine it had in it, what year, etc.) that I figured I should really learn about cars. My thought was this, "well I don't want to look stupid not knowing anything about my own car and I do want to fix it up, so why not learn?"

I spent days and nights reading everything there was known to man about cars, Corvettes, repairing cars, electronics, etc. I was spending so much time reading up on cars that I was never interested in going to high school parties, trying drugs, or getting caught up with the wrong crowd.

After all my research, I decided that I wanted to start fixing up my Corvette. I decided I wanted to do everything myself since I had taught myself the basics of cars. However, very quickly, I found out that a 1987 Corvette is one of the most expensive cars to repair. Everything on a Corvette is roughly two times the price of everyday car parts. When I would read the price tag on Corvette car parts, I was like a deer caught in the headlights.

Due to the ridiculous mark up in car parts, my dad suggested that I start a business, make it legit, and get a discount on car parts. I didn't have the first clue what he was talking about, but I thought to myself, "No other kid I know owns their own business. So why not?" My father, my mentor as always, walked me through the process of starting a sole proprietorship in the state of Kansas. Twenty-four hours and one trip to the city of Topeka later, and I was in business.

Lefty's Auto Accessories was the name, and buying and selling aftermarket auto accessories was the game. My plan was to set up as an "out of my house" retail store that would buy aftermarket auto accessories solely for my 1987 Corvette. It wasn't too long after kids at my school started seeing the latest wheels, tires, and auto accessories on my Corvette that they started asking "Where in the world did you get that?" My reply, "I own my own business selling this stuff." Right then and there, I started selling aftermarket parts to other kids at my school.

It was only a matter of months until my friends told their friends, and those friends told their friends about Lefty's Auto. It was through this viral growth that I built a name in the Kansas City market for having "parts priced so cheap you'd think their stolen." This mass viral effect allowed me to create a rather successful business at a very young age.

Fortunately, I never had to work at quick serve restaurants or somewhere that was paying minimum wage. I learned real time, real life experiences about running a business. It was this experience of moving forward with my passions and dreams that motivated me for the next major step and next major goal in my life.

My Motivation – You Can't Do It

When I was a junior in high school my parents sat me down and said: "Mike, we would like to see you become as successful as possible and we would really like for you to leave college debt free. Therefore, however much school you can finish in four years; we are willing to pay for. Plain and simple." This was a very interesting concept. In theory, I thought I could probably finish undergraduate school and graduate school in four years. But why not sooner? If I could do it in four, why not three?

Since this was somewhat of a challenge for a naive 16 year old to comprehend, my mother, a very intelligent high school teacher, said she would help me plan for college in such a way that would allow me to finish my undergraduate degree in just two years. This plan would involve no Advanced Placement classes (AP classes) but would require years of relentless hard work at both my local community college and my Big 12 school of choice, the University of Kansas (KU).

I was motivated to plan ahead with the help of my mother and finish my undergraduate degree in just two years out of high school. But what really motivated me was the amount of people that said I was full of manure and that there is no way on earth that I could accomplish what I was trying to do. Even my junior year English teacher said, "Mike, it's nice to have goals, but don't let yourself down by creating ones that are to big for your britches." This "you can't do it" attitude fueled my fire so strongly that it turned me in to a machine that was determined to accomplish its goal. Since my goal was set, it was time to put in the hard work.

My Hard Work

The plan was to finish my undergraduate degree in two years. In order to do this, we estimated that I was going to have to transfer roughly 50 credit hours of prerequisite courses from Johnson County Community College (JCCC) over to the University of Kansas (KU). I started taking basic courses at JCCC that would without a doubt, transfer to the University of Kansas and count toward a business degree at KU.

Every semester and summer since I was a junior in high school, I started taking on campus and online classes that would count toward a Business Administration degree at the University of Kansas. This allowed me to cram roughly a total of 45 *completely transferable* credit hours to KU upon high school graduation. This made me just a few hours short of being labeled a "junior" at KU before I even stepped foot on campus. What this really meant was that I would never have to take the classes that students labeled as "the drop out classes" at KU. I maneuvered around that by taking those drop out courses at JCCC and not KU. The even better part is that because the classes all transferred, so did my GPA. You've got to love that.

While at the University of Kansas, I made sure I took no less than 18 hours of on-campus classes and no less than 3 hours of online courses during any given semester. All of the classes I took were courses that could transfer as "liberal arts credits" that would count towards that specification of my Business Administration degree requirements. Cramming all of these hours was really not that hard. Taking classes that were not my core interest online was the key.

I even had some time for a little overseas travel. The summer after my freshman year at KU, I studied abroad in Paderno del Grappa, Italy, in conjunction with the KU business school. This allowed me to take nine credit hours of business courses while studying in a beautiful Italian environment. We went to school Monday – Thursday and then traveled all over Europe on our free time from Thursday through Sunday. It was the greatest experience of my life, and I suggest anyone reading this book to schedule in a little overseas education during their college experience.

Last, but not least, after feeling the bliss of graduating from the University of Kansas in just two years, I transferred to the University of Missouri – Kansas City (UMKC) to obtain my Masters in Business Administration. UMKC is a 60 hour or two year MBA program, which is standard throughout the public educational system. Fortunately for me, UMKC allows you to finish an MBA in 30 hours or in just one year if you have an undergraduate business degree from an accredited university. So in my instance, all it took was two semesters of 15 hours a semester. This, of course, was a breeze since I remembered the undergraduate days of 21 hours a semester.

The best part of all is that I managed to finish my degree in two years while having a good time and being a regular kid. While in high school I was the captain of the track team, I was a state pole vaulter, I was the President of DECA (a high school business club) and I hung out with a very close group of friends that I still spend time with today. Despite all the hard work and crammed classes, it was never too much to be athletic and have fun.

My Success

On May 7, 2006, just three years after graduating high school, I accomplished my goal of earning not only my undergraduate degree in two years, but also earning my graduate degree in just one year. The feeling of accomplishing a goal that took over five years to plan and implement is beyond explanation. It must be experienced in order to fully understand the emotion, relief, and pride felt at that point in your life.

Don't let this small story of success blind the true hardships and real work that became apparent along the way. It was a tough road with many pot holes that yielded opportunities for failure. I have had more sleepless nights, life changing experiences, failed tests and barely passed classes than I should have encountered. These memorable experiences of college are what have molded me into the hardworking motivated man that I am today.

Where has all this taken me? After graduation with my MBA I ran my own marketing consulting company, Fuzzy Media, Inc. for nearly one year. After long consideration and 100 hour work weeks, I decided to end my Fuzzy Media venture and take an opportunity to become the lead Marketing Manager for a very prominent commercial kitchen equipment manufacturer named Power Soak Systems. I now run and continually develop a lean and world class marketing operation at a premier small business in Kansas City, Missouri. It is a dream job that allows me to put all of my skills, talents, and interests to work.

Without the push and motivation of my parents, this would not have been possible. All the time you hear that the most successful events in life are not achieved single handedly. It is very difficult to move forward with a goal or plan if there is no cheerleader around letting you know what you are doing is right. This is why I constantly thank my parents for always being there to support me and to guide me into the light when all others were hoping for me to fall into the abyss.

Keep this in mind whether you are a student, teacher, or parent. You need someone to believe in you as much as you believe in your own dreams and aspirations. It will fuel the fire to your ultimate success.

YOU CAN'T DO IT
THE MOTIVATION

You Can't Do It

If you read the title of this chapter and said to yourself "you're right," then that's the first thing keeping you from finishing college on time. Success in college and in life is contingent upon your attitude and level of motivation to follow through with the things you desire. Whether it is staying up all night to finish a paper, walking in zero degree arctic-like weather to the library, meeting a study group at a friend's house, or taking a summer to catch up on classes, you have to get motivated at some point in time to do what is necessary in order to reach your ultimate goal: graduation.

Get Motivated - Even if it's just a little

In order to get motivated you have to first ask yourself, "Why am I going to college? Is it to party and have a good time? Is it to ultimately graduate with a bachelor's degree and then move on to a good paying job?" Take 10 seconds to think about that.

If ten seconds have passed and you can't tell yourself why you want to go to college, then you need to really spend some time thinking. It's not bad that you don't know. In today's society, it is almost a necessity to earn a college degree in order to land a good paying job, to advance in a challenging career field, and many times, to be socially accepted. Additionally, there is also a lot of social pressure from parents, students, and teachers to attend college that sometimes creates students who go to college and have no idea why. The fact that you just know you want to go to college is great. But, you need to figure out why YOU are REALLY going to college if you ever want to finish on time or finish at all.

If you are going to college in order to get away from your parents and party, chances are you won't finish on time, you'll drop out. Dropout rates are at a staggering 50% for incoming freshman and not showing any improvement. I've seen firsthand just why the dropout rates are so high and the answer is simple. There are enough levels of sinister temptation that if you don't have an end goal in mind, you will flush your college career right down the community toilet.

This concept is simple. Would you rather run around a track until someone tells you to stop, or run 10 miles? Neither of those choices sounds fun to me, but I would rather run 10 miles. That way at least I have a goal and know there is an end in sight. Point made. It is much more difficult to get motivated about something when you don't have an end goal in mind.

Day Dreaming Isn't So Bad

The first step to figuring out what you want to do is day dreaming. That's right I said it. When you're bored in math class, work, in the car, or in my case, Spanish class, day dream about what you love most. Day dream about where you would like to be when you're 30 or what type of lifestyle you wish to live. Just know, whatever you're day dreaming, that's the direction you need to head.

Some scholars say that you should do whatever you would do if money wasn't a problem. If money wasn't an object what would you do? Fish all day, be a painter, play drums? That way of thinking, *in my opinion,* is backwards. The fact is, money is an issue and too many people go to college either not knowing what they want to do, or picking something so generic that 1/3 of the entire campus has picked the exact same career path: Thus, making it impossible to find a job when they leave college and enter the working world.

What do I suggest? Here is my philosophy: choose something that will make you happy and will provide you with stability (an earnable income). Lots of things can make you happy and guess what? Statistics show that people change career fields more than three times throughout their life time. So really, it isn't set in stone what you are going to be doing for the rest of your life. But you do need to know what makes you happy so you can set your goals toward that choice.

For instance, I enjoy business. The whole concept and structure of business fascinates me. When other guys are watching ESPN and staying up to date on who has the most hits/strikeouts this season, I'm spending my time reading Forbes, researching business strategy, technology, and more. I also enjoy organizing things, I enjoy graphic design, I enjoy traveling, and a slew of other odd things in life.

So for me, when I was 16, I decided I was going to get a business degree. I didn't know what I wanted to do in business (marketing, finance, operations, etc.)

but I knew that I was fascinated by it and that I could earn a living in business.

The best way of choosing a career that has ever been described to me was by a Kansas City entrepreneur named Joe Roetheli of Greenies Chewable Dog Treats. You know, the guy that invented the little chewable dog mint called "Greenies." At the 2007 UMKC Entrepreneur of the Year Award dinner, he said to me, "Do what you want your gravestone to read, not what will drive you to the gravestone."

He went on to explain,"imagine yourself floating in heaven just after you passed away. Now imagine what your gravestone reads. Do you want it to read, "Here lies Mike Wilson, a miserable and unhappy accountant of 40 years" or, "here lies Mike Wilson, a happy, successful, family oriented businessman." I couldn't help but laugh.

A Real Life Example

You already know that I figured out what I wanted to do early in the game, but I bet you are wondering if there is anyone else known on earth that has? The answer is simple. Yes, a lot.

A very close friend of mine that I've known since I was in diapers realized when she was a senior in high school that she needed to escape the small, naïve world of Overland Park, Kansas and move to a much warmer climate. She played soccer and was good at it but knew she never wanted to be a pro star.

After finding a love and passion for editing film, she majored in it and finished college in exactly four years. When I asked her what motivated her to get done in four years, she interestingly stated "Thank god I found my passion for film otherwise I'd be a beach bum in Florida working at a restaurant and probably living with my friends. Then, of course, I would never have the chance to be on my own and live my own life." My only response was, "Well put."

Having Your Own Life

Having your own life someday should be one of the main reasons why you want to go to college and ultimately graduate on time. It feels fantastic. Having a good paying job that finances life's necessities and any luxury that you might desire is nirvana.

The sooner you finish school (say, four instead of five years) the sooner you will have the opportunity to start a life of your own. When you start your own life, you will have the opportunity to begin making a real sustainable income that will support the lifestyle you wish to live, or to start saving money for a house. For some people it may mean that you will have less money to pay back on student loans.

All reasons to get it in your head that you just need to figure it out.

FIGURE IT OUT

Be Your Own Advisor

Figure it Out

The first and the very most important step to finishing college on time is figuring out what field you are going to major in and STICKING TO IT. Whether it is business, accounting, mechanical engineering, art, or teaching, you have to know what your end goal is going to be. Sounds pretty simple but too often people are pressured into majors that they aren't interested in simply because they think the career field will be "cool" or it will pay a lot of money.

Then around sophomore year of college when students start to grow up and begin to realize they have to make decisions that will impact the rest of their lives, they freak out and change their majors to something more convenient. This costly decision is a small, yet significant, reason of why only 33% of college students finish in four years. Please don't make this mistake. Figure it out.

What is Required? The Purple Book

Once you have figured out what degree you wish to obtain, take it into your own hands to figure out what classes are required in order to graduate on time. To figure what classes are required, you need to go to the college of your choice, march into the respective major's building (i.e. business building, engineering building, math building, etc.), and walk right in the front door of the student services office.

In the student services office they will have pamphlets outlining to a T what you have to take, what elective courses are acceptable and what grade point average you must have in order to be accepted to the school of (business, engineering, education, etc.) The guides or "the purple book" as I referred to it at the KU business school, is your written proof, guideline, and Bible to legitimately finishing in four years or less.

If you visit my website www.Thruin2.com and click on "resources," you will find an exact PDF scan of the "purple book" that I picked up from the student services office at the University of Kansas business school in Summerfield Hall. As you will see, everything you need to know about what classes to take and what is required to graduate with that degree is covered in this one tiny purple book. Take some time and look through this book. You will want to find a tool similar to this book before you even step foot on campus. It will save you headaches, time, and, most of all, money.

(See the "Transferring to a Four Year College" chapter in order to figure out what you need to do at your local community college in order to transfer ALL of your credit hours to a four year university.)

Listen to Everyone, But Do Your Homework (Research)

Listen to as many people as you can about what classes you should take, what teachers to avoid, etc. Whether the advice comes from friends, family, or advisors, listen to what they have to say. Many of these people have been there, seen it, done it and have the t-shirt to prove it. They can provide very valuable information that you may not get otherwise.

However, when it's all said and done, you really need to do your own research as to what classes you can take, what is required for your major, when classes are available, etc. This is actually tough work and can sometimes be frustrating, but believe me, there is no other way to fool proof your college career. The more information you can find in official collegiate resources, the better off you will be.

Additionally, verify everything everyone says. Do your research via Google, word of mouth, your purple book, your blue sheet, etc. The reason for this is twofold. One, it is just smart, as you will learn to research things for yourself and make your own decisions. Two, student advisors are not ALWAYS right. Like many walks of life there are plenty of good student advisors that are genuinely looking out for your best interest. However, it seems that for every one fantastic student advisor you will find one who doesn't care, doesn't know, or acts like they know but really doesn't. In other words, be in control of your own destiny or the dagger of despair may strike.

Personally, I had terrible experiences with student advisors all throughout undergraduate school. I would go in and ask questions and receive a different answer from every single advisor, no matter what the topic.

How I ultimately got around the whole debacle was by walking in the student advising center door knowing exactly what was required of me via the "purple book" and the "blue sheet." I would then tell the advisor what courses I was thinking of taking and have him/her sign off that those classes would count towards my degree. This way in the end, I had everything documented.

So, needless to say, the gamble is yours. Be your own advisor, make smart decisions, and have people verify your plans and results, or risk the chance of bad information, a bad advisor, and not finishing on time.

COMMUNITY COLLEGE

Making Difficult Classes Easy

Community College

As I will outline in this chapter, there are some fantastic benefits to attending a local community college before attending a four year university. Keep in mind that even though I took over 50 hours of community college courses while still in high school, you don't have to do what I did or to the extent that I did it. You can take just a few hours in high school, you can go straight to community college right out of high school, take advanced placement classes, or you can go full bore like me. The choice is yours, but the concepts are applicable across all avenues.

Community College is Less Expensive Than a Four Year College

This is the number one most important thing to saving you thousands of dollars on your college education. Take the entry level prerequisite courses at your community college that you would be taking freshman year at a four college. This is even more important if you will be paying out-of-state tuition at a four year institute.

Let's compare three scenarios

The cost of 128 credit hours at the University of Kansas (equivalent to a business administration degree) vs. transferring 15 hours from Johnson County Community College vs. transferring 30 hours (or two semesters) of coursework from Johnson County Community College toward your degree. *(Note this does not factor in tuition rate increases, room and board as well as living expenses.)*

Four Year Business Administration Degree from the University of Kansas:

128 hours In-State Tuition @ $ 213 / hr = $ 27,264

128 hours Out-of-State Tuition @ $ 560 / hr = $ 71,680

Four Year Business Administration Degree from the University of Kansas including 15 hours (1 Semester) of JCCC transferable credit.

113 hours In-State Tuition @ $ 213 / hr = $ 24,069

113 hours Out-of-State Tuition @ $ 560 / hr = $ 63,280

15 hours at Community College @ $ 63 / hr = $ 945

Total Cost of In-State Route = $ 25,014

Total Cost of Out-of-State = $ 64,225

Cost Savings for In-State Tuition =$ 2,250

Cost Savings for Out-of-State Tuition = $ 7,455

Four Year Business Administration Degree from the University of Kansas including 30 hours (2 Semesters) of JCCC transferable credit.

98 hours In-State Tuition @ $ 213 / hr = $ 20,874

98 hours Out-of-State Tuition @ $ 560 / hr = $ 54,880

30 hours at Community College @ $ 63 / hr = $ 1,890

Total Cost of In-State Route = $ 22,764

Total Cost of Out-of-State Route - $ 56,770

Cost Savings for In-State Tuition = $ 4,500

Cost Savings for Out-of-State Tuition = $ 14,910

As you can see, there is an obvious cost benefit to taking prerequisite courses from your local community college rather than completing all your coursework at a four year institution. You can take as little or as many as you like, but do realize, the more classes you take at a community college, the lower your overall educational costs will be.

Community College is Easier Than a Four Year College

It's not that you learn less when you take courses at a community college. It's just that a community college is meant to be a resource for *the community*. You will have plenty of non-traditional students and working professionals who attend your local community college who are not looking for the intensity of a four year university.

This is especially important if you're someone like me, who has always been a low A / B or high C student and had a rough time with standardized tests and large classroom environments. Fortunately, for me, I managed to take Biology I, Calculus I, Micro Economics, Macro Economics, Western Civilization, and Literature I all at Johnson County Community College. If you know anything about freshman year at a Big 12 university you will realize that I just listed the top 5 "dropout" courses for incoming freshman.

I managed to get A's and B's in these courses without blinking an eye. This is because the classrooms were smaller, the coursework was lighter, and the testing was less standardized than what you will find at a large four year institution. Simply stated, unless you're a brainiac, take the tough courses BEFORE you go to a four year college and save yourself the headaches and the money.

Your Grade Point Average (GPA) Is Almost Guaranteed to Transfer

When you are trying to get accepted into the Business School, the Engineering School, etc. these "schools" will look at your college GPA up to that point in time. Now, after reading the first two sections of this chapter you will probably already have a good idea of what I'm about to say. Because the classes in community college are easier and because your GPA is almost guaranteed to transfer to your four year college of choice, you have an advantage over all the people who got lower grades than you taking the comparable courses at the four year institution.

For instance, if I had the exact same course grades as Adam Smith, EXCEPT, I got B's in Microeconomics and Western Civilization at Johnson County Community College and Adam Smith got a C in Microeconomics and a C in Western Civilization at the University of Kansas; I have an advantage over Adam simply because my GPA will be higher.

When it's all said and done, and you go online to check your "college GPA" you will see that your GPA is mixed with your community college grades and four year college grades. What else can I say? It works to your advantage.

You Become Accustomed to the College Work Style

Moving away from your parents, being totally free for the first time in your life, trying to meet new friends, trying to learn the campus layout, trying to find out the best pizza delivery in town is simply enough to drive anyone mad; or, in many cases, simply enough to drive over 50% of college freshman to failure. After failure comes officially dropping out and then moving back home with your parents. Please DO try to avoid this. It is embarrassing and pride smashing for everyone I know who has been faced with this life altering juncture.

One nice part about community college is you learn what it's like to take college courses. They are not going to be as hard as a four year institution, but you will learn what teachers look for, what college professors styles are, how to work with teacher's assistants (TAs) and even more important what college midterms and finals are like.

Getting in this "college work mode" is key to making the freshman year transition as smooth as possible. So save yourself the shame of dropping out and moving back home. Take classes at your community college.

ONLINE COURSES
The Best Kept Secret

Online Courses

If you take nothing from this book other than the following fact, I will have succeeded. Online courses are education's best kept secret. Hands down, without a doubt.

What a great and innovative concept online courses are and what an asset they have become to the students who utilize their wizardly powers. Here is the concept: a student can study at their own pace anytime, anywhere, any day of the week and be tested on the skills / lessons they learned through online reading, classic text-based reading, online discussions and web-based projects.

Knowing this, here are the three biggest reasons why you should incorporate online coursework into your college schedule.

Online Courses Are Easy If You Have Self Motivating Work Habits

There are two kinds of people. People who know how to work hard and those who don't. Knowing how to work hard isn't a skill you are born with, you learn it through years of experience. That said, if you are one of the people who know how to work hard or are motivated to become that way, online courses from a community college or even a four year institution are the EASIEST way to get a good, quick, easily earned grade.

Online Courses Allow Flexibility

The wonderful part about the 21st century, and online courses, is that you can do your coursework anywhere you want. Whether it's on your laptop with a Wi-Fi connection or at the school library, you can get access to your coursework and do your studying, and testing all mobile, at your leisure. Courses are structured so that you have a time frame to complete tasks or homework, but usually there is no set "universal" time that everyone has to sit down and take a test or turn in your homework.

You Can Take Online Classes Simultaneously With Other Course Work From a Different Institution

This is exactly what I did. I was a student at the University of Kansas and Johnson County Community College all throughout my college career. Later, I became a dual student at Park University and the University of Kansas. I was taking 18 credit hours at the University of Kansas and then at night breezing through literature classes online in order to complete my "humanities" requirements for my business degree. The entire time I was an official student at the University of Kansas.

A shocking (but later exciting) element of this arrangement was that in my last year at the University of Kansas, I found out that I could only transfer a limited amount of hours from a "two year" college. Most people would stop taking online courses at that point and start focusing on taking more classes at their current college. However, being the stubborn young man that I was, I developed a better idea that worked well beyond what I imagined.

To combat that this rule regarding courses from a "two year college," I started taking online courses from a different "four year" college, Park University in Parkville, Missouri. At Park University, I managed to take 15 credit hours of history and literature classes that all counted and transferred, without a loss of one single hour, to the University of Kansas. The even better part is that these classes show up on your transcript as traditional classes. They don't have any labels or codes that designate them as online courses.

How did I know what classes to take and which ones would transfer? Just like Johnson County Community College's "blue sheet," *(See "Transferring To A Four Year College")* Park University has their own bay of sheets that have official guidelines for courses that are available and which courses will transfer to what colleges. It's a handy little tool.

What Are Online Courses Like?

Online courses are structured in a variety of ways, depending on the class or the teacher, but are all essentially the same. Imagine them as virtual classrooms where you have windows of time to complete work and tests as opposed to one set, universal date. The only major difference is, you don't ever have to "go" to class. Here is some insight into what online courses are actually like.

You DO Have Books, Reading and Homework.

There will never be a way around having to do reading or homework as long as institutional education is the medium for advanced learning. However, the work load for online courses tends to be much lighter than what you will find in a traditional classroom. Many classes take into consideration that because the course is online you do not have the benefit of seeing a teacher face to face and learning content firsthand. They assume you have to teach yourself and because of this make the coursework much lighter. So, as mentioned before, if you know how to learn and retain information, online courses will be a breeze.

The resources and elements for online coursework are varied. Many times there will be online readings in PDF format, websites you have to visit, and sometimes you may have to go to the bookstore and buy textbooks just like you would in other classes. This all varies, but just understand that there are more mediums of obtaining information in online courses than just in textbooks.

You DO have to take tests

Tests for online courses can be taken one of two ways, depending on how the teacher organizes the course. Either you can take the course online through a website interface or you will have to go into a testing center and take the test on paper or by a standardized computer format. Either way, the tests are just like any other class. You have prep exams, study sheets, rules, time limits, etc.

However, do note that when you take a test online it is always open book and open notes. That means if you are going to have to take a test online you can review any resource you like, during the test, in order to answer the questions correctly. It's a pretty sweet deal.

Some Classes Do Require You To Participate In Discussions

My generation, Generation Y, is extremely technologically savvy. Because of this, institutions have started to integrate online discussion groups in a closed and specially formatted Internet forum. This forum format allows students to speak their mind on topics, philosophies, or research in a web-based and interactive manner.

Teachers then grade students on their level of participation and depth and breadth of their posts. Studies show that for Generation Y, online collaboration is usually the preference for voicing internal thoughts, expressions and opinions. It is much harder for a student to showcase their opinion on a topic in class room of 30-500 peers than it is to voice that same opinion in an online forum.

If you are a part of Generation Y like me, you know how much easier it is to voice your opinions and express your ideas without the fear or social retaliation in a classroom. In high school I hated voicing my opinion. Usually it was because my opinion was so deep or so off the beaten path that most students would try to shoot me down just because of the simple fact that it sometimes just didn't make sense.

However, when I started taking online courses in high school, I noticed I had a much easier time explaining and expressing those opinions somewhat anonymously, which ultimately helped me hone my in class room speaking skills. This is the exact reason why institutions are offering online courses. It's academic evolution.

SUMMER COURSES

Spend Your Free Time Adding Value

Summer Classes

What do you do during the summers between school years? Work, travel, do nothing? Take classes? Many of you will think "go to classes" and laugh. Isn't summer supposed to be the time when I relax and forget about school? The answer is yes and no. I always viewed summer as a time when I should take school *less* seriously. Summer was a time when I could take two or three courses at Johnson County Community College in a four to eight weeks and get ahead of the game. Why sit around and do nothing during the summer when I can add value to my college career now?

Summer Courses Are Easier

Summer courses, like many of the other things I have discussed in this book, are often actually easier than regular coursework. They are more intense as far as the workload due to their short length, but most teachers understand that it is summer and that, in truth, most of their students really don't want to be in class. In summer classes you will find an abundant amount of students who either failed that class a semester before or missed enrollment and are now having to take the class during the summer in order to catch up. So, you are ahead of the game if you are in summer classes because you want to be there.

Six to Eight Week Course Length

The other part that makes summer courses so great is that you can take an entire semester long courses in about a quarter of the time. Classes range from six weeks to ten weeks in length and usually try to cover the same work load as a regular semester.

However, if you have ever actually been through a summer course, you will know that many times, teachers will skip sections or topics that may be unnecessary in favor of getting through more important subjects.

International Summer Courses

The greatest experience of my life was having the opportunity to study abroad for a summer in Paderno Del Grappa, Italy, through the University of Kansas Business Program. The summer study abroad program lasted for six weeks and all classes were taught in English by an array of accomplished professors from all over the United States. Each student had a variety of classes to choose from and could take up to six hours of coursework during the six week period. I chose Finance and International Human Relations (two classes that I knew would be easier in a summer program).

The true hidden gem of the study abroad program went way beyond the easier course work and beautiful historic scenery. Classes were only held

Monday through Thursday afternoons. Then on Thursday afternoon, everybody was free to travel to where ever they like for the entire weekend. The weekend was everyone's opportunity to make a four day weekend trip, traveling to the most desirable places in all of Europe.

My weekend ventures took me to Florence, Rome, Barcelona, Milan, London and many more. The sights I saw and the experiences I experienced were beyond my initial comprehension. Hands down, I value my travel experiences in Europe as the most eye-opening and street-smart building encounters in my entire life.

I strongly suggest anyone who has the opportunity to spend at least one summer studying abroad. It is worth it.

Transferring To A Four Year College

Transferring To A Four Year College

If you are not already in college, then you're lucky. You can start researching and may get something done a little early. If you plan on attending a community college before you transfer to a four year college, then you need to take your research beyond the "purple book."

One of the biggest problems with attending community college is that quite often your credit hours are not accepted at the university you are transferring to. When this happens, it is money wasted and time wasted. Often people cry in agony and sorrow and contemplate quitting. So, not only make sure you make a site visit to you future college and get a "purple book" but then make the following actions happen as well.

What is Required? The Bay of Sheets

Go check out the "bay of sheets" (as I liked to call it) at your local community college, in my case Johnson County Community College. At pretty much every community college in the United States, in the student advising area, there will be a large organized stack, or bay, of paper sheets for hundreds of colleges and all of the respective majors at those colleges. They will be in all different colors and are usually in a central location. These sheets are as identical in purpose as the "purple book."

These sheet(s) are your guide and Bible for making sure you take the EXACT classes necessary in order to transfer ALL of your credit hours to your college and major of choice.

For a Business Administration major at the University of Kansas, my sheet was blue. Of course I referred to as "the blue sheet." By picking up one of these sheets you will not only be documenting and verifying that you are taking the correct transferable classes, but you will have a guide to making sure you stay on track and never deviate. If followed correctly, the "blue sheet" is almost a pre-formed four year class schedule.

I spent a few hours before every semester planning which classes I should be taking the following year. College is like a chess game. In order to win you have to look a few moves ahead. What classes should I take after this semester? What are a couple of fun classes I can take to fulfill my general education requirements? All rudimentary questions, you should ask yourself.

Once again, if you visit my website, www.ThruIn2.com and click on "resources" you will find an exact PDF scan of my JCCC blue sheet. Take a few moments to review this. You will see that the blue sheet will tell you exactly what courses will transfer as prerequisites for that specific degree.

It Does Work

Due to proper planning, a helpful mother, and a few hours of thinking, I managed to transfer in the ballpark of 50 credit hours to the University of Kansas as an incoming freshman.

Technically this labeled me as a sophomore in college that was just few hours short of junior status. What this allowed me to do was begin taking courses right away that I actually wanted to take. Doing this made me much more motivated and willing to work hard in order to finish ahead of time.

Imagine how much more motivated to finish school on time you will be if you got to go right into college and skip Western Civilization, Literature I and Pre-Calc. Do yourself a favor, jump the gun a little in order to make your world easier during the best time of your life.

Graduate!

Don't Forget To Graduate

There is no possible way to understand how good it feels to graduate from college until you actually do. It is a feeling of total relief and overwhelming joy. For many people, like me, it is the first time in their life that they have succeeded at a goal that has been with them for more than four years.

In order to earn the right to graduate, for many schools, there are many stipulations and a lot of fine print that sometimes is not always visible. I know many students who were allowed to walk at graduation but still had to come back for an additional summer or sometimes even an additional semester because they were just a few classes short of their total required credit hours. This is also a major reason why such a high number of students don't finish their degree in four years anymore. Apply the following actions in order to avoid making this mistake.

Make Your List and Check It Twice

The best way to make sure you are finished with college when it comes time to graduation is to double check your respective school's course requirement book (i.e. the purple book) during your JUNIOR year of college. If you wait until senior year of college to double check that you have fulfilled the requirements, it will, many times, be too late.

Furthermore, every year as you go through college, be sure to make one of the school advisors sign off on your record that the courses you have taken will apply to your future degree. Many times, over a four year period, some classes may change and no longer count towards a specific degree. So, unless you have an advisor sign off that you took those classes prior to the new rules, you may wind up accidentally losing credit for those courses and in turn having no way of proving yourself.

Fill Out The Graduation Paperwork

When you get to your senior year of college, many advisors will tell you that you need to fill out paperwork in order to be listed in the graduation directory, to get your diploma, etc. Even though every student gets an extremely advanced warning that they need to fill out this paperwork and turn it into the student advising center in order to officially graduate, there is always a handful of individuals who blow it off or just simply forget. In turn, they don't graduate. So, don't be careless and forget to graduate.

A Two Year MBA In One Year

A Two Year MBA in One Year

A Masters in Business Administration is one of the most highly regarded graduate degrees one can earn in their educational career. In recent years, an MBA has become almost a standard requirement for upper management and executive level positions with medium to large size companies. An MBA is a degree that many people desire but very few have the time, money, or will to endure the hardships and workload that are associated with the degree. An MBA is priceless.

With that in mind, know that there are two main types of MBA programs in the graduate education world that are equally the same and viewed no differently. The Traditional MBA Model and The Non-Traditional MBA Model.

The Traditional MBA Model

The Traditional MBA model is a two year program consisting of 60 credit hours which requires full days on campus with loads of coursework based around the "case study method."

The case study method, in a nutshell, is the process of taking a look at a variety of real world business "cases" and analyzing the process, results, and methods behind the given situation. The traditional MBA model is very time consuming, very rigorous and many times is much harder to get into than a non-traditional MBA Program. However, programs at many of the most prestigious schools like Harvard, Yale, MIT, Stanford, and Wharton are all based on the traditional MBA Model.

The traditional MBA Model states that regardless of whether or not you have a background in business or you are new to the business world (i.e. getting an MBA with a background in law, English, etc.) you will have to take 60 full hours, or two years, of courses (there are always exceptions, of course).

Let's say you have a background in business from an accredited college and because of this you have fulfilled many of the "first year" MBA prerequisites. Instead of "comping out" of (i.e. skipping over) these courses, you must take higher level courses than the other students and still complete a total of 60 credit hours. Not to say this is bad, however it will push the flexibility and capacity of your mind to the limits over those two years.

The Non-Traditional MBA Model

The non-traditional MBA Model is a two year program consisting of 60 credit hours which has focused its attention to the "non-traditional" student.

The non-traditional MBA student is generally characterized as a student who is a working professional by day but dedicated to getting their MBA at night. This type of program usually consists of night classes Monday through Friday with lighter workloads than your traditional MBA Model. The work load is lighter simply because the program is oriented itself the working professional that gets off work at 5:00pm and has to be in class at 5:30pm.

The non-traditional MBA Model makes the assumption that if you are coming into the MBA program with a background in business from an accredited college, you may "comp out" of, or literally skip over, any prerequisite courses where you qualify.

For instance, if you have an undergraduate Business degree from the University of Kansas, Kansas State University, the University of Texas, or many other accredited colleges and you want to get your MBA from the University of Missouri - Kansas City, you can comp out of up to 30 hours of coursework. This will ultimately leave you with just 30 hours of additional coursework in order to obtain your MBA.

This is the path I took for the sake of time, money, and principal. I went to the University of Missouri - Kansas City (a top 10 entrepreneurship school) and was able to comp out of 30 hours of coursework due to my Bachelor's in Business from KU. Since I was a recent graduate and not a working professional, taking 15 hours of coursework per semester would be no problem for me and that is exactly what I did.

I picked up a part time job during the day with the Kauffman Fellows Program in order to pay for everyday living expenses and then went to school at night. The coursework was easy for me, compared to my undergraduate coursework; however, what I learned in my MBA was invaluable.

My MBA Experience

An undergraduate degree is like getting an unassembled bicycle with a poorly written instruction manual. You know how to ride a bike, you just can't figure out how to get the thing built. You are overloaded with information from the instruction manual and you can't decipher anything it says. Even if you did get it built, there's no way you could ever tell someone else how to assemble a bicycle. Getting an MBA is where you learn how to build the bike.

With that said, I feel that I would not nearly be as capable of a businessman as I am today without my MBA experience at the University of Missouri - Kansas City. I loved my undergraduate years at the University of Kansas, but I left school having a hard time figuring out if I could apply anything that I had learned over my two years there.

Not to say that my undergraduate degree was worthless. What my undergraduate degree taught me was how to work hard, how to research answers to complex problems, and how to acquire large amounts of information and process that information into a useful a resource. This is a skill set that is hard to come by without having the experience of earning a bachelor's degree from a four year university.

However, where I feel the real value was provided to me was in my MBA program. I thrived and shined at the University of Missouri - Kansas City MBA program. What the MBA program taught me is almost beyond explanation. I learned the process of being creative and managing creativity, how to network and build business relationships, how to manage people, personalities, and work place indifferences. Most of all, I was taught how to teach myself.

The MBA program at UMKC taught me how to expand my mind, open the barriers and learn the complexities of the business world and in life on my own. These remarkable lessons are things I will always value and never forget.

I strongly suggest that you look into getting your MBA if you want to go beyond lower level employment and into middle or upper level management. The soft skills an MBA will integrate into your repertoire will always be valued by not only you, but by your employers and peers as well.

Maximize Your College Career

Maximize Your College Career

College is supposed to be fun. Millions of people worldwide refer to college years as the time of their life, reminiscing about days when life was more carefree and harsh realities were not yet apparent. College is where you meet friends for life, eat as much as you want, stay up as late as you want, and pretty much for the first time in most people's lives, do whatever you want.

By taking the time to be a college student, have fun, and experience campus life, you will not only have an overall better college experience, but you will find that your grades and your stress level will be at a much more desirable level.

Take Some Fun Courses

I took a few fun courses that actually counted towards my degree. My two favorite courses were Tennis (one credit hour) and Earthquakes and Natural Disasters (three credit hours).

Tennis was a one hour course I took my last year at KU that enabled me to have exactly 128 credit hours (the amount of total hours necessary in order to graduate). Our class met two days a week and learned the fundamentals of playing tennis. By the end of the course, even a student with the tennis skills of Napoleon Dynamite was able to serve like Andre Agassi. It was easy, it was outside, and it was fun.

Another course I had a blast in was Earthquakes and Natural Disasters. The man who taught the class was a hoot and the course had a reputation for being fun and easy. The course was focused on the science and history behind the world's natural disasters. Filled with incredible images, light hearted science, and tons of jokes, this course is a legend on the University of

Kansas campus. The course was three credit hours and fulfilled a humanities requirement for my degree. Every campus will have a class that is fun and easy and will count towards any degree. Find yours!

Go To Your College's Sports Games

I'm not just talking about tearing down goal posts after your football team beats your rival (which I've done - twice) or even about rushing the court after your basketball team knocks out the #1 team. What I'm talking about is going to see some of your school's smaller sports teams.

I loved going to the girl's soccer team games. Aside from the fact that I had a very close friend who was on the team, I found girl's soccer fascinating because so many of the players were villains and assassins on the field but sweethearts on campus. I always got a kick out of watching the girl's soccer team at KU nearly break out into a fist fight with a rival team. It was pure, simple fun that I still remember as a highlight to this day.

Another really fun sporting event that I went to was track and field. Going to the track and field events was fun for me because I pole vaulted in high school and had a friend that was on the University of Kansas pole vaulting team. What makes going to the event even more exciting is the fact that college track and field is a breeding ground for professional athletes. It is like watching a free pro sporting event. It is truly captivating.

So whether it is basketball, football, soccer, track and field, rowing, tennis, boxing, or swimming, go to a few of your college sporting events. It will make college a lot more enjoyable.

Follow Up on Your Campus Lore

Every campus will have some form of a legend or lore that only a handful of brave students have dared to research.

At KU there always has been a legend about "underground tunnels" that connect all the buildings on campus. Some say they were built for teachers to go from hall to hall without having to go out in the cold, others would say that they were built during The Cold War as a safe underground passage way in the event of nuclear war.

All these campus stories about the tunnels are just myths to most of the school population. The problem was, no one knows where the tunnels are located. The University of Kansas has them hidden and even if you do find them, they are locked. That is, of course, except for the elite few that did some research and found them on their own.

I am one of those elite few that managed to find the underground tunnels myself. I stumbled across them on my way to campus one day only to find that the gates and doors were locked. Later I found a secret way in through a hidden entrance behind a stairwell in the middle of campus. Could it have be something legitimate like a maintenance area? Maybe. Maybe not. If you go to KU, check it out for yourself.

The point is, if I didn't follow up on the campus myth, I would not have had the fun and joy of saying I was one of the very few to find the tunnels. So check into the campus lore, it feels good to know firsthand.

Do I Regret Anything?

The one question I get asked the most is, "Don't you feel like you missed out on anything by finishing college in two years?" My response is no. I lived college to the fullest knowing that I only had two years. I took every opportunity to travel, meet new people, go to basketball games, or out on dates. To me, it was just a part of going to college and I loved every minute of it.

Many students with lofty aspirations in college sometimes forget to be what they are: college students. Whether you are studying to be an aerospace engineer, a doctor, a teacher, or even a businessman, don't forget that the time you spend in college will probably be the most care free and fun times of your life. So enjoy it.

Do's and Don't's

Don't Be Scared

Just because I threw out a large sum money for college and a bunch of statistics about how the bulk of students fail, don't let that scare you. Chances are, if you picked up this book or if it was given to you by someone you know, you are the type of individual that will succeed in college and in life.

You would be amazed at how many people, if told about this book, would more than likely not take the time to read it and soak in the facts and tips. That's what separates a winner from a loser, a leader from a follower, or more importantly a graduate from a dropout.

I can recall many times in my college career when I was completely scared out of my mind wondering if I was going to finish college in two years or if I was even going to pass a crucial class. I can't tell you how many nights I laid in my bed wondering what in the world I was going to do in order to pass a class. That is how hard I struggled with my college career.

However, what got me over being scared and on to being confident, was confidence in myself. I knew that I could put my nose to the grindstone and work my butt off in order to pass a class. If you know you can work hard, be passionate, and put forth the effort to succeed, you should never have anything to be afraid of.

Don't Be Discouraged

The University of Kansas Masters in Business Administration Program was my first choice. KU was my Alma Mater and where I considered home. Getting into their MBA program was my only dream and part of my plan since I was 16 years old. The only problem was, the University of Kansas didn't want me.

The University of Kansas Masters of Business Administration Program would not accept a student of my age (20 at the time) who did not have two years "post graduate" experience under their belt. Owning your own business, strong letters of recommendation, and a competitive GMAT score was not good enough to secure a position in the KU MBA program.

On the flip side, the University of Missouri - Kansas City welcomed me with open arms -- literally. Once UMKC found out that an early graduating, hardworking, entrepreneurial student was looking to attend their school, they were as welcoming as family waiting for you outside an airline terminal after a long flight. In my only year at UMKC I was named the 2005 Student Entrepreneur of the Year and my picture was used for a UMKC Business School ad campaign. It was all a shock and still is a surprise when I think about it.

Beyond my personal success at UMKC, I can't count the number of times a UMKC MBA teacher would ask before class, "Who here does not have a job?" There would always be one or two embarrassed souls who would raise their hand. After a few seconds the teacher would tell them to visit with them after class and they would find them find a job. And they did.

Every time a student said they were jobless, one of the teachers would set them up with a decent paying job, either with a local business or through the University. UMKC's warmth and open doors shocked me and made me realize that there are schools that value things beyond what's on paper.

So don't be discouraged if you don't get into the undergraduate or graduate school of your dreams. Things always work out for a reason and always steer you toward a path that was meant to be. Even if you don't see it at first, you will later wonder how it could be any other way.

Do Be Brave

Being brave is one of the most important components to succeeding in college. Whether it is asking an advisor for help, calling your parents or friends for advice, going into a teacher's office to ask questions, or choosing a career path that may be a difficult and frustrating track to success, you need to have the guts and courage to step up.

Believe it or not, the hardest thing for me was attempting to make friends and join study groups in college. The biggest problem was the fact that I was three to four full years younger than anyone in any of my classes. I was 19 and everyone around me was 22 through 24. Because of the age gap, I was always nervous that people in my classes would view me differently if they knew how old I was and, as a result, I would be labeled as "the nerd that is finishing school in two years." What got me over being shy and worried was simply being brave and confident enough to go out on a limb and start making friends.

In college making friends has a lot of benefits. Not only does it make the time go by faster and more pleasurable, but friends in classes can help you learn the material you don't understand. Furthermore, if you are a well connected individual, you will always get your ear on insider information about the test, you will get copies of that course's previous tests, and, as a whole, you will be a lot more prepared for tests, homework, and classes than you could ever imagine.

Do Be Optimistic

One of the hardest things to do is be an optimist when you are stressed out, frustrated, or intimidated. When you are working your way through college, just remember that there is a light at the end of the tunnel. And if you stay on track, that light at the end of the tunnel isn't a freight train, its freedom.

It doesn't matter if you're applying to a college, building a class schedule, or taking a test, you need to be optimistic and confident in what you are doing. Always remember that things could be worse and that you really aren't that bad off. You're in college and you are working your way to becoming an extremely capable human being and, even more, a very capable earner.

Do Be Prepared

The one word that can sum up a successful college student is prepared. I'm sure you have heard it a million times from teachers and parents, but it is the realest statement on this planet. Being prepared with information and resources will not only get you ahead but it will save your butt in a pinch sometime down the road. Being prepared will allow you to ace a test, finish college on time, never miss an assignment, and, even better, help you save an exorbitant amount of time and money in college.

Lucky for you, by picking this book up and reading it, you have taken a few huge steps to being prepared for college and to finishing on time. The information, tips, and guidelines provided for you in this book are some that will put you ahead of the crowd and make college much easier than you could ever imagine.

Summary

Summary

Just picture, one out of every three students you know will not finish college in four years. As high as 50% will drop out in the first year and either move back home or change to another college. This is a tough picture to imagine. However, I am willing to bet on the fact that if you have made it this far in my book, you will not be one of those three that doesn't finish on time.

Why Haven't You Heard This Information From Anyone Else?

The reason why these statistics are so staggering is that no one has been willing to sit down with or write to the student population about what steps are necessary in order to finish your college degree on time or even early. College is confusing. It is a conundrum. Until now, no one has tried to speak directly to the students and provide insight into the speed bumps, road blocks, and one way streets that exist in the post-secondary educational system. Additionally, it is not in a college's financial interest to have every student finish on time or even early. So, chances are you won't hear this type of advice from them either.

However, if you read this book, you will be one of a few elite individuals that have an edge on the system and your peers.

It's Easy - You Can Do It!

The information provided in this book is easy to implement and applicable no matter which college you are going to, public or private, east coast to west coast. If you really think about it, if an average human being with average test scores, with a mid ranking in his high school class, and no advance placement classes to his name can finish college in two years, then you can do it in four or less. Chances are good that if you're reading this book, you have a higher ACT score than I do. So don't be discouraged or intimidated, you can implement the hints, tips, and tricks outlined in this book. If you do, it will save you not only thousands of dollars but a lot of headaches, sleepless nights, and unsolicited stress.

Figure It Out and Stick To It

Such a big part of your success hinges on you figuring it out and sticking to it. Figuring out what degree you want to shoot for in college and not changing majors your sophomore or junior year. The earlier you know about what you want to do, the easier it is for you to prepare, and organize for that degree.

If you're going to be, or already are a freshman in college, no worries, you've still got time (but not a lot) to figure out what you want to strive for. However, if you wait much longer to make a decision, your chances of getting shot down like a clay pigeon -- are greatly increased.

Start Taking Classes at Your Community College

Recognize the money and stress you can save by just taking a couple of classes at your local community college. If you were to just take one entry level course like Western Civilization at your local community college, this book will have paid for itself many times over. Go to your local community college and visit the "bay of sheets." Take a look at the classes you can take now and just do it. They are easy. Much easier than what you'll find when you go to a large university.

Take Online Classes

For the sake of your sanity and for the sake of getting easy inexpensive credits that you can directly apply towards your degree, take some online classes. They are self paced, light work and most of all, a breeze to finish. Taking online classes will allow you to catch up on courses, cram three more hours into your schedule and sometimes even help you when you are in a pinch.

Take Summer Classes

At some point in time you have to take more than 15 hours a semester or you have to pick up two extra classes in the summer. That is just the way the college math works. So take a summer and get ahead or catch up on classes. The classes are shorter, faster and easier. If you really want to enjoy the summer while taking classes, study abroad. Not only will you learn and get credit, but you can travel the world in the process.

Transfer All of Those Credit Hours

If you do decide to take a few courses at your local community college or even spend your first year or two at community college, make sure that you don't throw any money away by not being able to transfer credit hours to the school of your choice.

Go to the four year school of your choice and get the degree requirements book that every school has posted. Then match that book with your community college's transfer sheet. After reviewing the two thoroughly, don't deviate from those sheets of paper (even if Yoga sounds like a really cool class). If it doesn't count towards your degree then its money wasted. If you want to see real life examples of the "purple book" and the "blue sheet" then visit my website at www.ThruIn2.com.

Don't Forget To Graduate.

Enough Said.

Stupid Actions Lead to Real Life Consequences

Partying your butt off, skipping class and falling into the sinister temptations of college will lead you to the road of a drop out. It doesn't take long. Usually within the first year if your grades are not acceptable by the college's standards, you WILL be put on probation or kicked out of the university. I can personally give you a list taller than Shaq containing the names of all the people from my graduating class in high school that either dropped out or were put on academic probation and ultimately kicked out.

Know that college is a struggle, that's the point. If you succeed in getting your college degree it says a lot of your character and to your goals in life. No one can take your education away from you once you have it. That is why employers and people value it so much.

Don't be a statistic, go to class and stay out of trouble. Make not only the people around you proud but work hard and realize that when you are done with your college education, you are free!!

Have Fun

Don't forget to have fun. Stressing over college will happen all the time. It happens to all of us. So, make sure you take the time to go out and find some of the smaller quirkier things that make college, college. Follow up on campus lore, go to sporting events, spend time with your close friends and most of all do what you makes you happy.

What Do You Get By Applying Things In This Book?

If you were to just take one course at a community college, this book will have already paid for itself. If you were to take one course at your local community college and one course online during your college career, then this book will have saved you a few headaches and a few hundred dollars.

If you read this book and learned enough to understand what it takes to finish in four years, this book will save you over $25,000 per year by not becoming a fifth or sixth year senior.

Now if you were to really apply this book and take just four courses at your community college before you graduate high school (two summers), take a summer or semester to study abroad (one summer), take two online courses during your school year and enjoyed yourself, you will be just shy of two semesters (one year) early for graduation. This means you can have the option to take the last semester or year easy or just graduate in three years. This route will have saved you over $75,000 by not becoming a "senior citizen" graduate while allowing you to travel the world and have a good time without any major stress.

No matter whether you are paying for college yourself or your parents are paying on your behalf, finishing college on time is a no brainer. Or it should be. You should want to get done on time, or even early, for the sake of your life, career and personal enjoyment.

Either way, on time or early, the tips and information provided in this book will give you the knowledge to do what YOU want to do with your college career without having to overpay or overstress.

Small Things That Save a lot

Organizational Items

Making A Schedule

Making a schedule may be one of the biggest components to helping you get organized and believe it or not, actually help you save time and money. Whether you are tracking your classes, your tests, when homework is due, when you're meeting with groups or even when you are going to meet with your teacher, a schedule is a necessity.

I always preferred to make a full schedule in Outlook or Sunbird (free desktop calendar) and print it out and put it on my wall. That way I could always look at my schedule. I also always synced my phone with my Outlook so I would know what my week looked like in school and so I could keep track of when homework was due. Believe me, from time to time, it was a life saver.

Google Calendar

It wasn't until I graduated that Google Calendar started becoming extremely popular. However, now that it is well known and highly regarded, I suggest that if you don't have a laptop or a smart phone, then use Google Calendar.

Google Calendar will allow you to do everything you could do on a desktop calendar; however, the most unique part is you can share multiple calendars with classmates, you can invite someone via email to an event on your calendar and get real time feedback of whether they are coming or not. Last, but not least, you can actually have text message reminders sent to your phone about any events on your calendar.

Google Talk

Another great tool you can use to help stay organized is Google Talk. Many people just think it is the Google version of AOL Instant Messenger. That's not exactly the case. Gtalk, as its coined, allows you to easily and elegantly have microphone to microphone conversations, transfer large files, and leave voice messages sent to one another. Where Gtalk would come in most handy is when you are working on large files like PowerPoint projects or Photoshop files collaboratively for school projects. Gtalk is faster, easier and more reliable than trying to transfer a few hundred megabyte file over campus or even personal email.

Laptops

Laptops are a student's best friend. When I was in my second year of college, laptops started becoming extremely popular on campus due to their drastic price decreases. Now, you are almost not a legitimate student if you do not have a laptop in class.

The greatest part about laptops in college is that you can work from anywhere you please. No longer are you attached to a physical location like your dorm, your apartment or the library. Many people, like myself, are either on the go all the time or hate being confined to one physical location.

So this means you can send emails, type a paper or even research pretty much anywhere you can get Wi-Fi connectivity, which is nearly everywhere.

Furthermore, laptops allow you to take fast notes in class, add deadlines immediately to your calendar or give you the capability to research in-depth a concept that you don't understand in class.

Here's the best part. Laptops are now cheap. Dell offers deals by the week on student oriented PC's, online distributors are always slashing prices, and finally computer companies are finally offering extremely cheap laptops. So, invest in a laptop, it will be your best friend.

Productivity

OpenOffice.org

Sun Microsystems (a large software company) blessed the world with a free alternative to Microsoft Office called, OpenOffice. OpenOffice(.org) looks, feels, and functions almost exactly the same as Office 2003 / XP. Additionally, it opens and saves Word, Excel and PowerPoint files and runs on all major operating systems including Windows, Mac and Linux. OpenOffice.org is licensed as a free desktop program and has been downloaded more than 98 million times. Therefore you know it's popular. So, take a chance at using OpenOffice before you spend the money on an expensive Microsoft Office Suite. This entire book was written in OpenOffice.

AcademicSoftware.com

The wonderful part about the 21st century is that technology and software companies have finally recognized the large difference between students, regular consumers, and business. The result of this differentiation is websites like AcademicSoftware.com began popping up offering heavily discounted computer software to certified students and teachers. Check out their website before you ever think about buying something retail again.

Thunderbird / Sunbird

Thunderbird is a free desktop *email* alternative to Microsoft Outlook and Sunbird is a free desktop *calendar* alternative to Microsoft Outlook. Thunderbird allows you to seamlessly download your email messages from multiple accounts (i.e. campus email, personal email, etc.) and reply back via whatever account it was sent to. The nice part about Thunderbird is that you can quickly go back and look at emails that were sent to you without having to be online.

Sunbird on the other hand is a very basic desktop calendar program that allows you to import public calendars, publish your own calendars and keep track of your own calendar in real time. Just like

Thunderbird, you do not have to be logged into a web interface in order to check or add anything to your calendar. It is a fantastic tool for managing your school related schedule.

Firefox

The only reason I bring up Firefox is that it is a free, yet more secure alternative to Internet Explorer. When you are on campus you will find that there are more opportunities for hackers, spyware and malware to gain access to your computer than you could ever image. So if you care about the longevity of your laptop and not having computer crash two days before a paper is due, then download and install Firefox. It runs on all operating systems.

External Hard Drives

One thing that will save your life is an external hard drive. Connecting to your computer via a USB port, external hard drives can store all your data, papers, pictures and projects with the peace of mind that you will never lose your data to a hard drive failure. It's easy to use and works just like your computer hard dive.

Let me give you a real world example of why you need to back up your computer to an external hard drive. I was in MicroCenter (a computer store) looking around for a new monitor when I walked by the "service center" and saw this poor girl in tears screaming, "Whhhhyyyyy?" The interesting part was her tears were not one of those everyday "I'm stressed out and need to vent" kind of tears they were the hysterical, "My Dad just died" kind of tears. Poor girl.

The embarrassed and distressed girl then proceeded to say, "What do you mean you can't get my paper off my hard drive?" I cringed by having knowledge of her plague.

When the girl left I asked one of the guys at the counter what happened? Yes it sounds geeky, but I do know people that work there. As the story goes, this girl had a behavioral psychology research paper *ready to print* on her MacBook and all of a sudden, "BOOM!" the computer shut down and wouldn't restart.

What happened was a virus finally caught up with her computer, the hard drive over heated and shut it down. The result? A completely fried hard drive. Talk about the irony of life.

There are measures to restore the data and upload it on to a new computer, but it was going to take three business days for MicroCenter to do so. The worst part is; the paper was due THAT NIGHT. Teachers don't care if you had a hard drive failure. "That's life," as a college professor would say. She was basically out of luck.

I feel sorry for her, because I know plenty of people who have been in that exact same place. This all could have been solved if the girl would have backed up her files to an external hard drive. Plain and simple.

Don't think it will happen to you? Well according to StudentBackUp.com, "50% of all computers experience failure and data loss and 70% of students NEVER backup." Think about that the next time you are typing that monster research paper.

Books

Buying Books

Buying books from a store is never an issue. You can always find them in stock and you can have them in your hands within minutes. However, if you really want to save some money, go to the book store and get a look at what the books you are going to purchase looks like. Then go online to Amazon.com or Google Search the book title. You will find, generally, you can get the same book for roughly 50-75% of the price. This means you can save usually a few hundred dollars per semester just on books. Try it out; believe me it's worth the hassle.

Returning / Selling Books

The biggest money making scheme in collegiate history is when bookstores buy back your books from the previous semester. Here is how it works. You buy a book at $100. At the end of the semester they offer to buy back your book at $20. They then resell that book next semester to another student at the same rate at which you bought it, $100. So they roughly make $80 each time some student buys that book. You have no control on the purchase price of the book and are, therefore, at the mercy of the bookstores.

However, if you're ultra smart, you will buy the books either online or in a bookstore and then attempt to resell that book to another student at a price higher than the buyback rate from the bookstore but lower than the bookstore retail price. Say $80.00. Make a posting on Facebook of what book you have and what class it is required for and it is almost a guarantee someone will purchase your book(s). This way you don't lose as much money at the end of a semester.

Research

Google

JFG. Just Freaking Google It. That is the best piece of advice I can give you when you are trying to learn some concept from a book that is beginning to absolutely frustrate you. Google is the world's greatest invention that allows you to find useful and easy to understand information in seconds. It's simple, if you don't understand The War of 1812. Type it into Google. If you don't understand how businesses are valued. Type in "business valuation methods" into Google. Googling anything you don't understand will greatly increase your knowledge base and will help you be much more prepared when it comes to test time.

Wikipedia.com

Even though Wikipedia is not considered an official reference source for papers, because anyone can edit a wiki article, what Wikipedia does the best is explaining in simple and plain terms what exactly you are looking for.

If you want to use Wikipedia in a paper, go to the page that you want to view (ex: Donald Trump) and go down to the very bottom where it says "Links" or "References." Click those links and then read those articles. These are the articles that you can cite and use in referencing to a paper. This will save you days of time over a given semester.

Dictionary.com

Very quickly and easily you can find out the definition of a word or an elegant alternative to it. Plain and simple, Dictionary.com is the official online dictionary and thesaurus. Use it. It will add value to your papers and to your writing.

Exactly How Much Can You Save?

Exactly How Much Can You Save?

Taking a look at the following information will give you a good understanding of not only how much money I saved, but how much money you could save by finishing on time or even early Do note that these are rough estimates based upon a variety of actual and researched data. *(Disclaimer: If you get easily bored by reading finances or math, skip this chapter.)*

I have compared the following educational routes.

1. **The Thru in 2 Route**

   How much money it actually took for me to obtain a Bachelor's Degree in Business Administration from the University of Kansas as well as a Master's Degree from the University of Missouri - Kansas City with all my transfer credits factored in from Johnson County Community College and Park University?

2. **The Four Year Route + 2 Year MBA (In-state Tuition)**

   How much money it would take for you to obtain Bachelor's Degree in Business Administration from the University of Kansas as well as a Master's Degree from the University of Missouri - Kansas City by doing the traditional route of four years at a "four year college" and two years for an MBA?

3. **The Four Year Route + 2 Year MBA (Out of State Tuition)**

   How much money it would take for you to obtain Bachelor's Degree in Business Administration from the University of Kansas as well as a Master's Degree from the University of Missouri - Kansas City by doing the traditional route of four years at a "four year college" and two years for an MBA?

4. **The Six Year Route + 2 Year MBA (In-state Tuition)**

   How much money it would take for you to obtain a Bachelor's Degree in Business Administration from the University of Kansas as well as a Master's Degree from the University of Missouri - Kansas City based on how long a typical student takes to finish college. Six years for a Bachelor's degree and Two Years for an MBA?

5. **The Six Year Route + 2 Year MBA (Out of State Tuition)**

How much money it would take for you to obtain a Bachelor's Degree in Business Administration from the University of Kansas as well as a Master's Degree from the University of Missouri - Kansas City based on how long a typical student takes to finish college. Six years for a Bachelor's degree and Two Years for an MBA?

(see next page)

Overview Comparison

A. Total Cost of Thru in 2 Route

= $60,126 (My Route)

B. Total Cost of Instate 4yr Degree + 2yr MBA.

= $98,534

C. Total Cost of Out of State 4yr Degree + 2yr MBA

= $162,014

D. Total Cost of Instate 6yr Degree + 2yr MBA

= $126,675

E. Total Cost of Out of State 6yr Degree + 2yr MBA

= $210,975

Total Cost Savings

Total Savings of A over B.................... = $38,408

Total Savings of A over C.................... = $101,888

Total Savings of A over D.................... = $66,549

Total Savings of A over E..................... = $150,849

A) Thru in 2 Route

OVERVIEW

Total Cost @ JCCC=.. $4,728

Total Cost @ ParkU =...................................... $4,120

Total Cost @ KU = ... $31,019

Total Cost @ UMKC =..................................... $20,258

Total Cost of Schooling =............................ $60,126

BREAKDOWN

Johnson County Community College

Credit Hours =.. 56

Tuition Rate / Credit Hour =......................... $63

Total Tuition @ JCCC =.................................... $3,528

Total Semesters @ JCCC = ... 4

Cost of Books Per Semester (avg) =.............. $175

Total Books @ JCCC = ... $700

Room and Board =.. $0.00

(lived at home)

Total Other Expenses =..................................... $500

Total Cost @ JCCC = ... $4,728

Park University

Credit Hours =.. 15

Tuition Rate / Credit Hour =.................... $260

Total Tuition @ Park University = ... $3,900

Total Cost of Books at ParkU = ... $220

Room and Board = ...(factored in at KU)

Total Cost at ParkU = ... $4,120

University of Kansas

Years @ School =.. 2

Semesters of School =................................. 4

Tuition / Semester = ... $3195

Total Tuition =... $12,780

Room and Board / Semester =................ $3,480

Total Room and Board = ... $13,920

Books / Semester =.................................. $250

Total Books @ KU =................................... $1,000

Transportation / Semester = ... $220

Total Transportation @ KU =.............................. $880

Other Expenses / Semester = ... $435

Total Other Expenses = ... $1,740

Total Cost @ KU =... $30,320

University of Missouri - Kansas City (MBA)

Years @ School =.. 1

Semesters of School =...................................... 2

Tuition / Semester =... $4,164

Total Tuition =... $8,328

Room and Board / Semester =........................ $4,800

Total Room and Board =...................................... $9,600

Books / Semester = ...$250

Total Books @ UMKC =...................................... $500

Transportation / Semester =........................... $480

Total Transportation @ UMKC =....................... $960

Other Expenses / Semester =.......................... $435

Total Other Expenses =.. $870

Total Cost @ UMKC =..................................... $20,258

B) Four Year Degree + 2 Year MBA (Instate Tuition)

OVERVIEW

Total Cost @ KU =................................ .... $58,019

Total Cost @ UMKC =.............................. $40,515

Total Cost of Schooling =........................ $98,534

C) Four Year Degree + 2 Year MBA (Out of State Tuition)

OVERVIEW

Total Cost @ KU =.. $99,659

Total Cost @ UMKC =................................. $62,355

Total Cost of Schooling =......................... $162,014

D) Six Year Degree + 2 Year MBA (Instate Tuition)

OVERVIEW

Total Cost @ KU =.. $86,160

Total Cost @ UMKC =.................................. $40,515

Total Cost of Schooling =.......................... $126,675

Total Cost @ UMKC =.............................. $40,515

E) Six Year Degree + 2 Year MBA (Out of State Tuition)

OVERVIEW

Total Cost @ KU =... $148,620

Total Cost @ UMKC =.................................. $62,355

Total Cost of Schooling =........................... $210,975

Want To Find Out How Much You Can Save?

Do you want to find out how much it will cost for you to go to school, when is your targeted graduation date or even exactly how much you will save on college? If so, then go to www.ThruIn2.com and click the "Resources." There you will find links to information on everything from when your targeted graduate date will be, to how much you will save by doing different class scenarios and most of all exactly how much you will save vs. the average student. So check it out, it is a great tool.

Acknowledgments

FAMILY

My Mother – Cindi Wilson

More than anything I would like to thank my mother. My mother was the one who helped me plan all of my classes and sat me down to show me all the tips that I am now providing to you in this book. She was the one who always believed I could do something if I really wanted to and never did anything to hinder my dreams. Beyond academics, my mother has been an inspiration to me for both my optimistic attitude and as caring mother. Simply stated, without her, I would not be where I am today.

My Father - Rob Wilson

The perfect match to my mother, my Dad has been and will always be my best friend. He has encouraged and molded me into the man that I am today. Most of all, my father has always been the strong force reminding me to be strong, not to wimp out and to barrel through the obstacles that I am faced with. A man of a 1000 motivational quotes, he will always play a part in my life.

My Sister

I want to thank my sister for always having my back. No matter what the issue is, at the end of the day she is on my side. Always providing the honest truth, I couldn't ask for a better sister.

Grandparents

My grandparents have ways been the excited and proud family members. I can always expect for them to brag about their little grandson and how well he is doing. My grandparents lift my spirits and build my optimism.

TEACHERS AND SCHOOLS

Shawnee Mission South

I would like to thank the Shawnee Mission School District. In all of my years of school and all of my travels across the world, I have not found any high school educational systems as strong and nurturing as the Shawnee Mission School District. I thank everyone who is involved with the Shawnee Mission School District for making SMSD the most enabling and premier district of its kind.

Sandy Hermreck

There is no possible way I could go any further without thanking Sandy Hermreck, my high school senior English teacher. It was Mrs. Hermreck that taught me how to write, how to read abstract books, how to interpret abstract thoughts. Even more, she was the one who taught me and many other graduates of Stone Cold Sandy's senior English class, how to be chivalrous and a gentleman in the 21st century. Thank you Mrs. Hermreck.

Teachers at SMS

I have to thank the entire teaching staff at Shawnee Mission South who played a role in my education. I had a great experience at SMS and feel that a large bulk of my academic success is in the teachers that prepared me. Thank you to Miss Johnson, and Mrs. Sinkler for always inspiring me and believing in my crazy ideas. Thank You Miss Johnson, Tod Nafus, and Mercedes Rasmussen for their insight on this book.

John Gergacz

Thank you very much Mr. Gergacz. Beyond your hilarious classroom stories and antics you taught me that diversity of an education is the best thing possible. Even though I didn't believe you at the time, the University of Missouri - Kansas City was the best possible institution I could have gone to. Thank you, for your fun classroom sessions and thank you for mentoring me on my post college decisions.

University of Missouri - Kansas City

Thank You UMKC! You're institution is the future of world class education. I appreciate that you value students beyond what is on paper and more about who the student really is. Your education programs in business taught me more real life information than I ever could have asked for. I know that in time, you will be recognized as a top ten entrepreneurial institution -- in the world.

Walt Rychlewski and Larry Lee

Thank you Walt, for believing in me. Your large smile and unique laugh always pushed me to continue my research and to continue my passion as an entrepreneur and as a marketer. Thank You, Larry Lee, for connecting me the right people and for giving me valuable insight on UMKC and the business world.

Michael Song

Thank you for creating such a world class Entrepreneurship program. What you have done at

UMKC is phenomenal. What you will do with UMKC's Bloch school is beyond my imagination.

Johnson County Community College

Thank you for creating a phenomenal education facility in the heart of Overland Park. Without my education at JCCC, it would have not been possible to achieve my goal of "Thru In 2."

University of Kansas

Thank you KU. You have built a nationwide recognition in excellence and quality higher education. A degree from your college carries weight and is always regarded highly. Rock Chalk, Jayhawk, Go KU!

FRIENDS

Ted Hammond

An extra big thanks to Ted Hammond. The college roommate that taught a nerd how to be social. Also, thank you for your help with the shooting the video for the marketing of this book

Mark Churchill

Thank you for your inspiration as a person and as a Christian. I value you as a friend. I value your insight and your honest opinions. Additionally, thank you for your impressive photography.

Eva Saviano

Thank you, Eva Saviano. A talented and extremely gifted writer and editor who provided a level of perspective and insight on this book that was truly amazing.

OTHER

Tom Perkins

Thank you to Tom Perkins and Fotolia.com for the cover art for this book.

Visit

www.ThruIn2.com

For more resources, videos, information,

and purchasing options.

www.ingramcontent.com/pod-product-compliance
Lightning Source LLC
LaVergne TN
LVHW091006080826
845145LV00003B/1148

* 9 7 8 0 6 1 5 1 9 0 2 4 2 *